How to Book
Speaking Engagements
at Churches

D1270582

Daniel King

How to Book Speaking Engagements at Churches

ISBN: 1-931810-12-5

Copyright: 2010
Daniel King
King Ministries International
PO Box 701113
Tulsa, OK 74170 USA
1-877-431-4276
daniel@kingministries.com
www.kingministries.com

Table of Contents

Introduction

Over the past decade, I have spoken at over a thousand church services in North America. This averages out to two or more services a week, every week, for ten years. When I meet other traveling ministers, they frequently ask, "How do you keep such a busy schedule? How do you book speaking engagements at so many churches?"

This book is an endeavor to answer these questions. If you are a minister, I want to help you develop a speaking schedule packed full of ministry engagements. If you want to preach, there is no reason you should not be preaching somewhere.

People are hungry for God. Churches across America need good anointed preachers to teach, inspire, and motivate their people. If you will follow the principles revealed in this book, you should never lack for a place to preach again.

Chapter 1

The Law
of Relationships

Who you know will determine where you go. Stop and think about that statement for a minute. Your direction, your path, and your productivity are determined by the people in your life. The level of your success is in direct proportion to your relationships.

When I was just a toddler, my father was earning his Masters of Divinity at Oral Roberts University. Across the hallway from my parents' apartment lived Billy and Marianne Allen. My parents became good friends with them, and over the years, the relationship deepened even as the lives of the two families took different directions. The Allens pastored a denominational church, launched an independent church, became Bible school directors in Jamaica, and currently pastor Christ for the Nations Church in Dallas, Texas. My parents traveled as tent evangelists, became missionaries to Mexico, and currently serve in a Muslim nation. Throughout all of life's ups and downs, our two families have maintained a wonderful relationship.

Pastors Billy and Marianne invited me to preach at their church when I was just a teenager. Later, they gave me one of my first opportunities to preach on the mission field. To this day, they continue to support our ministry in every way they can. We love and appreciate them for their encouragement over so many years.

It is long-term relationships like this on which a ministry should be built.

The greatest secret to success in ministry is found in the word "relationship." Having the proper relationships solves all other problems. You do not need money; you need a relationship. With the right relationships, money is no problem. The right relationship can hook you up with an opportunity or an idea that will provide money.

In order to book speaking engagements at churches, you need to build relationships with pastors. The key to developing relationships with pastors is to go where they gather. Go to as many conferences as you possibly can. Go fishing where the fish are. Get to know pastors and they will invite you to their churches.

We should seek to establish depth in relationships, not just breadth. It is possible to know a thousand people without ever having a true friend. God brings some people into your life for a specific reason, some for a season, and some for a lifetime. Discern the difference in every relationship.

In ministry, we need three types of relationships. These three relationships are illustrated by the life of the apostle Paul. He had Ananias (a mentor who spoke into his life), Silas (a friend and co-laborer), and Timothy (a protégé).

First, you should have authority figures who speak into your life. In my life, this position is occupied by my pastor, my parents, and various Christian leaders. I listen to each of these men and women of God and follow their advice. Different leaders are quali-

fied to speak into different areas of my life depending on their area of expertise or wisdom.

You can learn from your own mistakes, or you can learn from the mistakes of others. By finding a good mentor, you can cut years off your learning curve. If you lack wisdom, you can either learn by trial and error (a slow, painful, costly process), or you can develop a relationship with someone who has already solved your problem and follow his advice. Find someone who has been where you want to go. Study successful ministers. Get to know them. Ask questions.

Second, it is vital to have friends who are on an equal level with where you are. By fellowshipping with close friends, you provide mutual support and encouragement. I have several friends who challenge me to do big things for God. Proverbs 27:17 highlights the value of such friends: *"As iron sharpens iron, so a man sharpens the countenance of his friend."*

Third, you should pass your wisdom on to a new generation. Your discoveries should not die when you do. Find some young men or women to train.

Each of us is a brick in the kingdom of God. Relationships are the mortar holding us together. If you are not connected properly, you are either a brick lying out in a field by yourself, or you are causing a weak spot in the building. When an earthquake comes, a wall without mortar will be shaken apart.

Relationships are for both the good times and the bad times. Meaningful relationships must be built during times of fun so when life's inevitable storms begin to blow, there is something to hold

onto. God has not called us to independence, but interdependence. You will see exponential growth in your life because of your relationships. One plus one does not equal two; in God's kingdom, one plus one equals eleven. Synergy comes from relationships. John Maxwell says, "Teamwork makes the dream work."

Relationships keep you going in ministry. Being a minister has been called "the most dangerous occupation on earth." According to some statistics, fifty-two percent of ministers are divorced; 1,500 pastors quit monthly. Only one in forty who graduate from Bible school retire as ministers.

Some ministers jump from place to place, never putting down roots, never forming lasting relationships. It is vital to have covenant relationships in your life. If you are in divine relationship, you should not casually break the connection. Value the relationships God has given you.

Everything in ministry is based on relationships; therefore, you must strive to develop meaningful relationships. At first, you will be able to count your important ministry relationships on one hand. Cultivate them. The majority of your time and effort should go towards maintaining and deepening those relationships. Eighty percent of your time should go into the top twenty percent of your relationships. Choose your relationships carefully. Ask yourself if you want this person to be in your future. Invest time, energy, and effort in key relationships.

It is not what you know but whom you know, or to be more precise, it is who knows you. You can say you know many people, but the true test of relationship is what your friends or acquaintances say about you when your name is mentioned.

Chapter 2

The Law of Friendship

My mother has friends in almost every city in America. Recently, she and my father drove from Texas, to New York City, to Chicago, and then to California and stayed at a different friend's house every single night for more than a month. My mother has carefully cultivated her friendships her entire lifetime.

To be successful in ministry, you must be a friend-raiser, not a fund raiser. Pastors will run away from you if you give the impression you are only after money. Endeavor to make friends with people. Once pastors know you, they will be more likely to invite you to their church.

Here are some ideas for making friends:

* Genuinely care for people.

* Genuinely minister to people. Once you have met someone's need, they will be happy to help meet your needs.

* Be interested in people. This means you need to listen more than you talk. According to John Maxwell, "People don't care how much you know until they know how much you care."

* Read *How to Win Friends and Influence People* by Dale Carnegie.

Chapter 3

The Law
of the Laser

A light bulb can shine a soft light around the room, but if you take that same light and focus it into a narrow beam of laser light, it can cut through walls. If you are focused, you will be able to accomplish a million times more than if you do a little bit of everything. Focus creates impact.

I once asked a young minister, "What do you preach about?" He replied, "I just get up and say whatever the Holy Spirit tells me to say." He explained that sometimes he preaches about healing, sometimes about the rapture, and other times about revival. This lack of focus does not inspire anyone to invite him to speak. He thinks he can do everything, but in reality, he is known for nothing. He is a jack-of-all-trades, but a master of none. If you try to be "all things to all people," you will usually be recognized as an expert in nothing.

Almost every great minister is known for his focus in a particular area. For example, when I mention Kenneth Hagin, what do you think of? Faith. Every time I ever heard Kenneth Hagin speak, he started by reading Mark 11:23-24. He is known for his emphasis on faith. Even if he preached a message on marriage, he began and ended by talking about faith.

Many other renowned ministers are also known for their particular areas of expertise. Whenever they minister, they most always share along the lines of their hallmark message. For example:

- Billy Graham is famous for preaching about "salvation."

- Oral Roberts is remembered for "healing."

- Robb Thompson is known for "excellence."

- Kenneth Copeland speaks about "faith."

- Mike Murdock talks about "wisdom."

- Marilyn Hickey has a mandate to "cover the earth with the Word."

- Bob Harrison is known for "increase."

- T.L. Osborn is the father of "crusade evangelism."

- Joyce Meyers is celebrated for helping women "enjoy everyday life."

- Hilton Sutton is an expert on "end-time prophecy."

As an evangelist, my focus is soulwinning. In every message I preach, I talk about leading people to Jesus. I live and breathe for soulwinning. I study many different subjects. I have even written books on many different subjects, but my number one subject is "souls." When you think about Daniel King, I want you to think about my goal to lead one million people to Jesus every year. This focus is what creates my difference, my uniqueness, and the reason a pastor should invite me to speak at his church. If a pastor wants his congregation to hear about soulwinning, then I am the man for the job.

You have a limited time on this earth to live. It is better to become an expert on one subject than to know a little bit about many subjects. Find one key message for your life and become known for your expertise in that area. A laser focus will make you memorable and effective. One author pointed out that if you spend

ten minutes each day learning about a particular subject, within five years' time, you will know more about that subject than anyone else on earth.

I greatly admire the ministry of Buddy Bell. For over thirty years, he has been known as an expert on the ministry of helps. If a church wants their ushers, greeters, and parking lot security to be trained, they call Buddy Bell. He has become known as "the pastor's best friend." The power of his ministry lies in his focus on one particular area.

Having focus helps you make important decisions, decide what to spend your time on, and choose your friends. Without focus, energy is wasted. Unfocused energy is what happens in a lightning storm. Ultimately, you can achieve more by doing less. Find one thing to do, focus on that one thing, and become the best in the world at doing it. It is better to do one thing well than many things poorly.

In his epistle, James warns us of the consequences of having a divided focus: *"A double-minded man is unstable in all his ways"* (James 1:8). If you try to do more than one thing, you will confuse people and none of what you do will be very effective.

Answer these questions: What is your assignment? What problem are you called to solve? Who are you supposed to reach? What is your uniqueness? What can you do that no one else is able to do? What is the primary focus of your ministry?

The answers to these questions will help pinpoint your hallmark message. Once you discover your niche, work hard to be an expert in that area. Study, learn, practice, and communicate it whenever you have the opportunity.

Chapter 4

The Law
of the Menu

When you go out to eat at a restaurant, the waiter takes you to your table, sets a glass of water in front of you, and then hands you a menu. That menu showcases the various offerings from that particular restaurant. If you do not like one certain dish at a restaurant, chances are you will like one of their other dishes.

A pastor may not want you in one area, but he may need your help in another area. They will look at the entire menu of what you offer. Speaking to the whole church on Sunday morning is not the only time you can offer value to a church.

Can you speak for the youth group or minister in the children's church? Can you take people from the church on a mission trip? Provide books for the church bookstore? Do a training session for greeters and ushers? Offer curriculum for small-group Bible studies? Hold a consulting session with the pastor? Speak at a special event?

At first glance, this law might contradict the Law of the Laser, but it really does not. Your ministry needs to be focused, but that focus can be applied to a variety of different areas within a church.

Chapter 5

The Law of the Servant

One minister requires first-class airplane tickets when he travels. He demands to stay in five-star hotels and asks for certain types of exotic snack food to be available. He sends ahead several staff members to set up his book table. He requests that at least three armor bearers from the church be assigned to carry his Bible and notebook and provide security. He refuses to come unless a certain size honorarium is guaranteed. Often his plane does not land in the city until after praise and worship has started in the church. To great fanfare, he walks out on stage, preaches, takes up an offering, and leaves before the people are dismissed. He acts more like a diva or a celebrity than a minister of the Gospel.

Meanwhile, other ministers are willing to travel to the middle of Africa, sleep on the dirt floor of a hut, and are equally happy to minister to a group of ten people or a crowd of ten thousand. If you are going to be a true minister, it is vital to have the attitude of a servant.

Jesus came as a servant. Matthew's Gospel tells us that He *"did not come to be served, but to serve"* (Matthew 20:28). Jesus said, *"The greatest among you will be your servant"* (Matthew 23:11). Whoever is willing to serve will be first in the kingdom of heaven.

For years I served my parents at their tent crusades in Mexico. As a teenager, I helped pound stakes for our Gospel tent, set

out chairs, and move the sound system. I lugged around boxes full of food to give to the poor. I passed out flyers to invite people and helped in any way I could. I learned how to be a servant, and this attitude has served me well as I have traveled to preach in churches.

Once, I was scheduled to preach in on particular church, but at the last moment, the pastor decided that another visiting preacher should share. He asked me to take care of the children instead. A celebrity would have refused, but since I am a servant, I accepted the change willingly.

All your publicity material should communicate your willingness to serve. You are not at a church to get something; you are there to give as much as you possibly can. Be a giver, not a taker. In God's kingdom, servants rule.

Paul told the Ephesian church to do *"the work of the ministry"* (Ephesians 4:12). This is because 90% of ministry is hard work. Only 10% of ministry occurs on the platform in front of people; behind the scenes there is a lot of hard work. Your willingness to serve by working hard is what qualifies you to be on a platform.

Chapter 6

The Law of Communication

Several years ago, I went on a mission trip to the African nation of Congo. While I was there, I met a young lady who was working as a crusade director for another evangelist. In the ten days that I was in Congo, we became friends. As I was leaving, I asked her for her email address. As I do with every email address that I collect, I added her to my email list.

Once she was on my email list, she began to receive my monthly emails. From time to time, she would answer my emails and give me a few details about what she was doing. After several months, she sent me an offering; that caught my attention. A year later, I went to Canada to preach at her home church. Because we had been corresponding, we reignited our friendship, and that week I asked if I could begin courting her long distance. We started talking on the phone, writing daily emails, and sending love letters to each other. Sixteen months later, we were married.

This story shows the importance of communication. If I had not asked Jessica for her email, she might never have remembered me. But because I communicated, our relationship was able to grow deeper. The same is true with your relationship with pastors. If people never hear from you, it is impossible for your relationship to grow deeper.

Out of sight is out of mind. If you do not communicate who you are and what you are doing, you have failed in a relationship.

If someone does not hear from you in a long time, they will forget who you are.

So take the time to communicate and connect with others. Email, call, send a postcard, or write a note. Your efforts to communicate will result in closer connection with pastors, mentors, peers, and friends.

Chapter 7

The Law
of Seven

If you do not have any success booking a meeting after contacting a pastor one time, don't get discouraged. It takes time to build relationships and trust. So keep encouraged and don't give up after the first contact.

It usually takes us an average of seven positive contacts with a pastor before he is willing to invite us to minister at his church. The first contact may be when we meet him at a conference. Then we start sending him our regular emails. Perhaps he responds to an email and orders one of my books. Then he begins receiving our monthly newsletter. I send him a publicity packet about our ministry. A year later we see him at another conference. I then give him a call and tell him we are scheduled to be in his area. Finally, he invites us to minister at his church.

A church that does not know you will not invite you to speak. You must tell pastors who you are. Tell them again. Remind them. Send an email. Send a letter. Keep telling them who you are, and eventually they will know you. Once they know you, you have broken down the biggest wall.

When a pastor begins to know you, you must build the relationship to a point where he trusts you. Once he trusts you, you must

offer him something he needs. Then he will invite you to speak at his church. It is a long process, but as you are faithful, the rewards will come.

Here are some ways to make positive contacts:

1. Develop a publicity packet. This should be the best quality you can afford. It can include video, a cover letter, résumé, or pictures. Do something unique to set yourself apart from the other thirty publicity packets a pastor will receive this month.

2. Ask for personal recommendations. Ask your friends to recommend you to their pastor. Word of mouth can be very effective.

3. Make phone calls. It is often difficult to actually talk with a pastor because of his busy calendar. Often it works best to talk with the secretary, send her an info packet, and eventually schedule a phone appointment with the pastor.

4. Set up personal meetings. Try taking pastors out to lunch. If you want to meet pastors, spend time where they spend time. This means going to conventions and special meetings.

6. Mail a monthly newsletter. Monthly exposure is great. For the cost of postage, you keep your name in front of people. This may not immediately pay off, but eventually they will start to recognize who you are. Weekly exposure through regular email updates may be even better.

7. Ask God to give you favor. Mike Murdock says, "A day of favor is worth one thousand days of labor." If God speaks to someone to bring you in, none of the other publicity contacts really matter. But even if God speaks your name to a pastor, and he's never heard of

you before, you probably won't get booked. This is why all the other contacts are so important.

8. Use social networks. Facebook, Twitter, YouTube, LinkedIn and email are all valuable ways of helping you connect with pastors. Use pictures and videos to communicate what God has called you to do.

9. Print a ministry brochure.

* Hire a graphic artist to design your brochure. First impressions are lasting impressions. Believe in your calling enough to invest in quality graphics.

* On your brochure you should include your photo, contact information (address, email address, website, phone number), credentials, vision statement, and a description of the topics you cover.

* Include references from well-known ministers who would recommend your ministry.

* Answer these questions: Why should a pastor invite you to his church? What value do you give? How can you minister to his people? What makes you unique? What would your ministry accomplish if you came to a church?

* Communicate your requirements for coming to a church. What do you expect in terms of finances, accommodations, and travel arrangements?

* Use the information from your brochure to create an 8 ½ x 11 sheet of paper that can be faxed or emailed to pastors.

10. Have a business card. If a pastor remembers your face, but does not know how to find your phone number, you have not fully communicated. Therefore, it is important to put your name, address, phone number, and vision on every piece of publicity material you give out. I was at a conference and someone handed me a book he had written. I liked the book and I wanted to contact the author, but nowhere in the book could I find a phone number, address, or website that would allow me to get in touch with him.

The Law
of Fruitfulness

Once upon a time there was a king. He was known far and wide for being good and just. The king desired to marry. He called his chief servant and said to him, "I want you to go to a kingdom far away to ask a beautiful princess to give me her hand in marriage. I am sending with you a priceless diamond to give her as a gift." As the servant traveled the long distance, he became extremely proud of being asked to carry the gift of the king. By the time he arrived at the palace of the princess, he was so puffed up with his own importance that he came across as arrogant. He threw the diamond at the feet of the princess and demanded she return with him to marry the king. Because of the servant's bad attitude, she declined. She said, "I like the gift you bring, but I don't like your heart." The servant bore the gift of the king, but he did not have his heart.

There are many ministers who are gifted, but the question you should ask yourself is: "Do I have the heart of my King?"

According to Paul, there are many different gifts the Spirit gives. He wrote about these ministry gifts in the epistle to the Corinthians: *"But the manifestation (or gifts) of the Spirit is given to each one for the profit of all; for to one is given the word of wisdom through the Spirit, to another the word of knowledge through the same Spirit, to another faith by the same Spirit, to another gifts of healings by the same Spirit, to another the working of miracles, to*

another prophecy, to another discerning of spirits, to another different kinds of tongues, to another the interpretation of tongues" (1 Corinthians 12:7-10). Some ministers are so enamored with their own amazing gift that they forget the Giver of the gift.

No matter how great your gift is, it is far more important that we have the heart of the King. Galatians 5:22-23 says, *"But the fruit of the Spirit is love, joy, peace, longsuffering, kindness, goodness, faithfulness, gentleness, self-control."*

The fruit of your ministry is more important than your gifting. It does not matter how anointed you are, how well you sing, or what amazing messages you preach. If you do not walk in the fruit of the Spirit, your ministry will always struggle. The greatest advice my pastor, Billy Joe Daugherty, ever gave me was, "Daniel, if you don't get bitter, you will make it."

When you exhibit the fruit of the Spirit in your life, your ministry will begin to bear evidence of great fruit like souls saved, bodies healed, and lives transformed. Jesus said, *"By their fruits you will know them"* (Matthew 7:20).

Many pastors want to see the fruit of your ministry before they will invite you to come speak. A fruitful ministry does not happen overnight. It is the result of years of dedication and obedience to God's commands. It is vital to develop a consistent and godly track record and reputation. When your ministry is fruitful, you bring glory to God. Jesus said, *"By this My Father is glorified, that you bear much fruit…"* (John 15:8). Start by bearing fruit at the level where you are. Communicate your fruitfulness; paint a vision of the future fruit your ministry can bear. Then ask people to invest in your future potential.

Chapter 9

The Law
of Persistence

When I was just getting started in ministry, I took one trip where I drove my tiny 1995 Geo Metro from Tulsa, Oklahoma to Houston, Texas to preach at a church. They gave me a $50 offering. Then I traveled into Louisiana for another service and received an offering of a couple hundred dollars. Finally, I drove up to Arkansas to minister for several days at another church that had about fifteen people. As I traveled, I did not have enough money for a hotel room, so each night I found a McDonald's and slept in the parking lot. As I lay there scrunched up in the back seat of my tiny car, the only thing I could thank God for was that my car was so small it got great gas mileage.

When a minister faces this type of situation, he has two choices. He can choose to endure, or he can give up and leave the ministry. The people who become great ministers are those who never give up.

Joyce Meyer tells a story about how she once traveled several hundred miles to speak at a women's Bible study in an old van with worn-out tires. When I heard her say she was forced to sleep in the parking lot of a McDonald's, I was able to relate to her story. Now God uses her to speak into millions of lives all over the world, but when she started, she thought twenty women gathered in a living room was a good crowd.

John Wesley traveled over 5,000 miles on horseback every year for fifty-four years. This is equivalent to traveling around the world eleven times. He preached over 40,000 times, an average of twenty sermons a week. Because of his persistence, there are Methodist churches all over the world.

In the formative stages of ministry, it's important to keep your focus. The first years of your ministry will be the hardest years in the area of finances. Make every penny count for the kingdom. Do not get distracted.

I have called some churches dozens of times before booking an engagement. Elisha told Naaman to dip in the river seven times in order to be cured from leprosy. If he had stopped after six dips, he would not have been healed. His persistence brought his miracle.

Most successful ministers are successful because they managed to hang on for the first few years of ministry. Mega-ministries do not spring up out of the ground; they are the result of years of hard work and experience. Set your eyes on the goal, put your hands to the plow, and refuse to look back. If you do not give up, eventually you will succeed.

Chapter 10

The Law of Value

Would you walk into a grocery store, give the cashier money, and walk out without any groceries? Of course not. If you give someone money, you expect to receive something of value in return. Why? Because if you give value, you want to receive value. The same is true of pastors. You will never receive an invitation until you provide something of value.

In life, you are rewarded based on the value you give. Different tasks receive different rewards. A lawyer is paid to solve one type of problem. A trash collector is paid to solve a different problem. Your difference creates your value. According to Mike Murdock, "Sameness creates comfort. Difference creates value." If you are the same as everyone else, you will be comfortable, but you will never be noticed. In order to give value, you have to offer a unique difference.

Every relationship must be based on the value you give. If you only focus on the value someone gives to you, you will be viewed as a parasite. You need to offer a unique value no one can find anywhere else.

According to the Principle of Reciprocity, you must give something of value before asking for anything. Zig Zigler says, "If you help enough people get what they want, you will eventually get what you want." If you are not offering value, why would anyone want to help you?

Remember, you are not trying to make money off pastors; you are trying to offer them something of value. Let's take a look at some of the valuable services you can offer pastors:

* Ministry. If you can minister to the pastor, his kids, or to a member of the congregation in a significant way, you have become valuable.

* Marketing. Can the pastor market you in a way that will bring new people into the church? Anytime you can draw people into the church, you have done the pastor a huge favor.

* Emotion. The emotion stirred up by someone giving to you can be of tangible value. People want to give to worthy projects, and they want to be emotionally and personally connected to what God is doing around the world.

* Opportunity for investment. The business mind looks for the best way to invest money. Offer value by being a good investment.

I no longer call myself a traveling minister or an evangelist because both of these terms have been abused. Now I am known as a missionary evangelist. A traveling minister is someone who comes to the church, takes up an offering, and leaves. But a missionary is someone who is sent out from a church to the nations. By telling people I am a missionary, I allow them to participate in reaching people all over the world. This is so much more valuable than just receiving an offering to pay for my personal expenses.

Ask yourself, "How many people am I going to reach? What country am I going to impact? How is my ministry bigger than myself?"

Chapter 11

The Law
of Salesmanship

I first started ministering at churches when I was still a teenager. My brother and I dressed up as clowns and did "Circus Family Nights" at churches across America. We juggled, rode unicycles, did puppets and comedy routines, and taught children about the Bible. When we began, no churches had heard of us. I simply picked up a phone and started calling churches and talking to pastors. It was a tough sell for a sixteen-year-old to convince a pastor to allow us to clown around at his church, so I was forced to quickly learn how to be a salesman.

I discovered the key to being successful in ministry is salesmanship. I would call pastors and ask, "Would you be interested in an exciting, fun-filled evening of family entertainment that would help you reach out to your community and bless your congregation?" I sold the pastor on the value of a clown show. Today, many of the churches we visited as clowns continue to support me now that I am an international missionary evangelist.

Zig Zigler says everything rises and falls on salesmanship. Every day, whether you like it or not, you are selling yourself, your vision, and your unique ministry. You are either doing a good or bad job of selling yourself.

Ideas to help you improve your sales:

* Read secular books on how to make sales. The wealth of the wicked is often stored in books.

* Practice sales techniques. If you had sixty seconds to convince a pastor to invite you to his church, what would you say? Do you know how to close a deal? Have you ever bought a car from a used car salesman? What did he say that made you want to buy his car?

* Be enthusiastic. If you are not excited about you, who else is going to be excited about you?

Sales is a numbers game. The more people you get in front of, the more sales you will make. If you build relationships with enough pastors, someone will invite you to speak. There are over 50,000 churches in America. Each church has three services a week. So, every week there are 150,000 church services. All you need is one or two services each week to keep you busy. God will tell someone to invite you. Keep calling. Don't be afraid to ask. If one pastor says no, there are another 49,999 churches out there to ask.

Chapter 12

The Law of Excellence

When I first started in ministry, I spent thousands of dollars on plane tickets to minister overseas, but I was only willing to spend ten cents to photocopy a black and white sheet of paper to mail to a pastor. I learned that if you want people to take you seriously, you must operate with excellence.

The clothes you wear, the shine of your shoes, the look of your publicity material, how quickly you return phone calls, the way you talk, and the cleanliness of your car and office all contribute to how people perceive you. Maintain a standard of excellence at all times, in all things. First impressions are lasting impressions. Go the extra mile. Be excellent in every detail at the level where you are, and you will make a good first impression. This will be vital in the years to come.

Be 100% professional in:

* Answering the phone.

* Returning calls.

* How you conduct yourself.

* The handling of finances.

* Your personal appearance.

* Keeping your word.

* Printing top-quality material.

Every day look for ways to increase your excellence. Ask yourself, "How can I improve the way I do things? How can I be a better minister? How can I increase order in my life?"

It is better to do one thing right rather than ten things half done. Excellence is doing the best you can at the level where you are. But keep in mind that your standard of excellence will continually be improving. Robb Thompson says, "Today's excellence is tomorrow's mediocrity." So continually strive for a new level of excellence every day!

The Law of Action

It is better to do something rather than sitting around doing nothing. There are thousands of people who have vision and who talk big, but there are only a few who actually do anything. Your actions are much more important than your good intentions. Your movement creates miracles.

So many people sit around waiting on God when, in reality, God is waiting on them. When you move, God moves. It is the steps of the righteous that are ordered by the Lord, not the sitting still. God cannot steer a parked bus.

Good things happen every time you minister, whether you receive an offering or not. Accept every invitation to minister, even if it is a small church or a church that will not give a big offering. I would rather speak at a tiny church than stay at home. If you are too big to preach in a small church, then you are too small to preach in a big church. I like what Buddy Bell says to pastors, "The only reason I have not come to your church is because you have not invited me."

There are many benefits that come from continual action. First, you get exposure. Eventually, someone influential will see you minister and will help promote you. This will never happen if you are doing nothing waiting for the big contact.

Second, you find new contacts. Those new contacts have the potential to become someone important in your life. Every time you minister, you widen your circle of friends.

Third, every time you minister, you get practice. Oral Roberts once said, "You have to preach a sermon fifty times before you have a good sermon." You are not ready for the big-time if you've only preached a sermon one time. My signature sermon is "The Secret of Obed-Edom." I have preached this one sermon over 500 times. I can preach it in my sleep because it has become part of me. Every time I preach this message, it impacts lives.

Fourth, you gain experience. Each time you minister, you learn something new. A new idea might come to you, or you may learn to deal with a new problem. Or you may meet new people. Someday, all this experience will come in handy. Great ministers are not born; they are created one ministry engagement at a time. Ministry is a journey, not a destination.

Fifth, you discover supporters. Who knows who will begin to support you? Even if you are only ministering to ten people, several of them may choose to support your ministry. Actually, a greater percentage of small groups will support you than big groups because the small group gets to know you more intimately.

Sixth, you get re-invited. The value of your relationship will become more and more apparent over time. But you will never obtain precious relationships without movement. As you move, step by step, you will reach your destination. For more information on how your movement will create a miracle in your life, I recommend you read my book *Move: How to Fulfill God's Will for Your Life*.

Chapter 14

The Law of Uniqueness

One time I heard a preacher who had recently graduated from Rod Parsley's school. As he preached, he threw a handkerchief over his shoulder, not because he was sweating, but because that's how Pastor Rod always preaches. No matter who you are or whom you learned from, don't try to copy someone else's style. Develop your own style. As John Mason says, "You were born an original; don't die a copy."

Did you ever see the poster with thousands of black and white penguins all headed in the same direction? In the middle of the pack, there is one penguin painted bright red. He is headed in the opposite direction. Guess which penguin gets noticed?

Be unique. Stand out from the crowd. Distinguish yourself by being different. Be one-of-a-kind, distinctive, matchless, irreplaceable.

Three ways to be unique:

* Develop a unique message. Preach one message and preach it well. Master one subject that distinguishes you. What great truth has God revealed to you?

* Develop a unique vision. Pastors want to hook up with the latest thing. Be exciting, be new, be unique, and communicate your vision differently. Be a pacesetter and a visionary. What are you doing that no one else is doing?

* Develop a unique style. Benny Hinn is memorable because of his theatrical style. Jesse Duplantis is remembered for his humor. Rodney Howard Browne is unique because the joy of the Lord breaks out when he is preaching. What will you be remembered for?

Chapter 15

The Law of the Double-Dip

Recently, I bought an ice cream cone. At the ice cream store, the second scoop of ice cream was cheaper to buy. The same is true when you visit churches. It will always be easier to rebook a speaking engagement at a church you have visited than it is to speak at a completely brand-new church.

Many churches we continue to visit year after year. It is always fun to return to these churches, because after several visits we become like family members. We know the pastor, his wife, his children; we see their church grow over the years; we pray with them through the hard times and rejoice with them in the good times. When we have developed a long-term relationship with a pastor, it is never a matter if he wants us to visit; it is simply a job of finding a date that matches both our schedules. Thus, it is vital to build and maintain a relationship with each church at which you speak.

How to guarantee you will be invited back:

* Be a great speaker. Shine when you are on stage; the best way to get invited back is to wow them when you speak. Work hard on honing your speaking skills and your message. Invest extra time in prayer to make sure you have an anointed word from God when you speak.

* Send a handwritten thank-you card after your first visit.

* Exceed expectations. Deliver more than you promise.

* Develop relationships with key people in the church.

* Update the pastor on a regular basis.

* Offer something new every six to twelve months. For example, you might want to send the pastor a CD of your powerful new message or your newest book and let him know you are available to come again.

* When you are at the church, pay attention to the details of your conversations. Learn the names of the pastor's kids, find out the pastor's vision, learn about his building program. Type these details into your database; if you do not record the details, it is likely you will forget them. Later, when you call the pastor, ask him about progress in these areas and let him know you are praying for him. This is a practical way to show you really care about his church.

Chapter 16

The Law of
Extended Networking

I ministered at one small church and received a relatively small offering that barely covered the cost of gas to travel to the service. But after the service, the pastor called me into his office and said, "Daniel, you blessed my people so much. I have some friends who should invite you to speak at their churches." The pastor gave me a letter of recommendation and called three other pastors on my behalf. One of his friends later became a significant blessing to our ministry.

It is said that each of us is only six contacts away from every other person on earth. This means that someone you know is friends with someone who knows someone who is connected to any person you want to connect with. All you need to do is find the right connections. Every pastor has a friend you need to know. Most pastors have a dozen pastor friends. If you truly offer something of value, he will be happy to recommend you to his friends.

As you network, ask pastors the following questions:

* Do you know any pastors who would benefit from my ministry?

* Can you give me their addresses and phone numbers?

* Could I use your name when I call them?

* Would you be willing to call them on my behalf?

After getting new contacts, follow up immediately. Call the new pastor and say, "Last week I ministered at so and so's church, and he mentioned you would be interested in looking at my material. Can I send you an information packet?" Then follow up on the contact.

Chapter 17

The Law of the Seed

When my parents attended Victory World Missions Training Center, a missionary came to speak to their class. Although my parents had little money, they decided to start supporting that missionary. For over twenty years, I watched my mother write out a check every month to that missionary and about twenty other ministries. My parents taught me the importance of sowing seed. Because they faithfully sowed seed into other ministries, God supernaturally provided for their ministry.

Several years ago, I was lacking speaking engagements during one particular period. I felt led to help one of my friends find a place to preach. I made several calls on his behalf and introduced him to several pastors. Immediately after I began helping him, my phone began ringing with invitations.

The seed you sow determines the harvest you grow. So plant seed in others who are doing what you want to do. The type of ground you plant seed into will determine the harvest you reap. If you want to be successful in a particular area of ministry, plant seed into others who are working in that area.

Read my book *The Power of the Seed*. It studies every Bible verse that talks about seedtime and harvest, giving and receiving, sowing and reaping. If you will give to others, God will give to you.

Practical Plan
for Success

Here are a few ideas to get you moving in the right direction right now.

1. Write down the names of 10 pastors you have met.

1. _____

2. _____

3. _____

4. _____

5. _____

6. _____

7. _____

8. _____

9. _____

10. _____

2. Call each pastor today.

Tips for calling pastors:

* Before you call, take a deep breath to help you relax.

* Smile when you are talking. Your smile will change your tone of voice.

* Speak clearly and distinctly. Avoid mumbling or muttering.

* Listen to what the pastor is saying. Instead of thinking about the next thing you are going to say, be attentive to what he is saying.

* Be friendly and positive.

* Be servant-minded. Communicate your desire to help the pastor as much as you can.

* Be enthusiastic and passionate. If you are bored with what you are saying, it will come across in your voice.

* Be nice to the gatekeeper, the secretary, or assistant who answers the phone. You will need his or her help and advice. The job of these individuals is to help the pastor keep his focus. First you must earn their trust, and only then will they will allow you through to their boss. Be kind and respectful. If you don't get through on the first call, ask, "When would be a good time to reach the pastor?"

* Be persistent. Keep trying.

* Ask questions. These help build the relationship and reveal a pastor's true needs. People like to talk about themselves more than they like listening to you. Your questions will reveal the best way for you to sell yourself. The one who asks the questions is the one in control of the conversation. Show genuine interest in the pastor.

Ask these questions:

- How long have you been a pastor?

- How did you know you were called to be a pastor?

- How did you get saved?

- What did you preach about last Sunday?

- Who was the last guest minister who came to your church?

- Which spiritual leaders speak into your life?

* Follow up on your phone calls. Mail out a package. Send an email. Put a date on the calendar to call again.

* Here is a script I have used when calling pastors:

Hello, my name is Daniel King. I am a missionary evangelist and I am excited about leading people to Jesus. Is your church interested in soulwinning?

I travel to churches all over the United States doing three-day soulwinning conferences. Our ministry would love to put some practical tools in the hands of your people to equip them to be effective soulwinners. We have found that churches that get excited about soulwinning often experience explosive growth. Is that something you are believing God for?

Our heart is to do anything we can to help your church become everything God wants you to be. Would you be interested in inviting us to minister at your church?

All we ask is that you cover our travel expenses and receive a love offering each time we minister. What date would be good for us to come visit?

* If the pastor is not immediately interested in inviting us, I ask, "Can I mail you some information about our ministry?" If they say, "I'll call you," I ask, "If I don't hear from you in a few weeks, may I check in with you?" Each time I call, I have another chance to make a positive impression.

* If you get their voice mail, be prepared to leave a short (less than one minute), positive, upbeat message. Your first voice message may not generate a call back, but it will provide a good opportunity to make a positive impression. When you leave your phone number, say it slowly and distinctly so they can easily call you back.

3. Send each pastor a letter or a publicity packet.

4. Call five days later and ask if they received the packet. Ask if they read the packet. The chances are they did not have time to look at it. Politely ask them to take a look, tell them you will call in another three days, and let them know you are available to serve them anytime they need help.

5. Call three days later. Ask them how you can serve. One of the ten pastors may invite you, but do not be discouraged if none of them do. If the pastor is local, ask if you can take him out to lunch.

6. Send them a monthly newsletter about what your ministry is doing.

7. Continue to call each pastor every few months. Eventually, some of these contacts will turn into ministry engagements.

Questions About Calling Pastors

Recently, a friend asked me some questions about how to book speaking engagements at churches. Below are my answers.

What do pastors think when I call? First, understand that you are one of ten traveling ministers who will call this week. Pastors are busy and they cannot invite every traveling minister to preach. Some might think they don't need what you offer. Others think they can't afford you. Perhaps they think you are too small to come to their church, or they think your ministry is too big to come to their church. So when you talk to a pastor, change his perception of you. If he thinks he does not need what you have to offer, you have to convince him your expertise is valuable and that you fit what he is trying to accomplish.

Sometimes when I call, the secretary won't connect me with the pastor. How do I get past the person who is answering the calls? Become friends with the gatekeeper. Complement her on her phone voice. Make her your ally. Keep calling back. Peter and Tamara Lowe share in *Get Motivated* that they called Ronald Reagan's office every week for several years before he consented to speak at one of their events. Every week they talked to his secretary until finally they booked him.

Ask if you can talk to the pastor. If the pastor is busy or absent, ask what time would be a good time to catch him. You could say, "I would love to send an email of my latest teaching to the pastor. Could I have his email address?" This gets you in front of his eyes.

Should I go to small churches, even if they don't give me enough to cover my expenses? I am willing to go to any church, no matter how small or how far away it is. My policy is that if I have the date available, I will come. Because I go to small churches, God opens up the door for me to preach at big churches. Often I find that small churches give a better offering than some bigger churches. God always provides for my needs, and I find that good things happen every time I minister.

How do you speak at so many churches? I have been booked solid almost every Sunday for ten years. It is rare that I do not minister somewhere each week. A variety of keys opened all these doors. I visit conferences and develop relationships. People hear about me ministering in one area and invite me to their area. Every open door helps open more doors.

How can I develop a better relationship with a pastor? If he lives near you, ask if you can take him out to lunch. Make sure you pay for his lunch. If he lives far away, give him a call and encourage him. Many times I call pastors, not to ask if I can come speak, but just to find out how they are doing.

What information should I send a church? You can put together a CD or a DVD for them to watch. But that costs money to mail, and often it gets thrown in the trash. Perhaps it would be even better to put clips of your preaching up on your website. If you are talking to them on the phone, you can say, "If you have your computer there in front of you, you can visit my website to hear one of my recent messages." Some people have told me that they won't have me visit if they have never heard one of my messages, but most invite me just because they like me.

When is the best time to call pastors? Usually Mondays are not good because, for many pastors, Monday is their day off. On Wednesdays, most pastors are preparing for their Wednesday

night service. On Fridays, pastors often study for Sunday morning. In my experience, the best time to call pastors is on Tuesdays or Thursdays. However, there really is no "best" time. Don't let yourself make excuses for not calling just because the time is "wrong."

What if my efforts to call pastors are not working? Do not get discouraged if a church does not invite you to speak. Churches have a limited number of times available for guest ministers to visit. In a typical week they may receive five or even ten packets from ministers asking to come speak. Obviously, they cannot invite everyone. Be thankful for every opportunity.

Questions about Offerings

What is the best approach when it comes to the honorarium or love offering? Do you ask for a specific amount? I never ask for a specific amount. I ask churches to take up an offering to help us do our international crusades each time I minister. Some churches are small and can't take up a big offering. Some churches are big but won't take up a big offering. Often I will talk about the vision of our ministry and mention what the offering will go toward right before I hand the meeting over to the pastor to take the offering.

After the service is over, I often ask the pastor to adopt me as the church's missionary. I say, "We would be honored to be your missionaries. Would you help send us out every month?" Some churches adopt us and send a monthly missions offering. Other churches adopt us and don't send any offering. Some just say, "No, we already have missionaries we support."

Do churches receive an offering or give you an honorarium? I let the churches do whatever they want. I prefer churches to receive an offering every time I minister because this allows

people to sow into world evangelism.

Do churches ever shortchange you on your offering? I have never known of anyone stealing any portion of my offering. Other traveling ministers have warned me that this happens, but if someone has done it to me, that is between them and God.

If a church gives me an offering, can I use a portion of it for my personal use or does it have to go completely to the ministry? In King Ministries International, our personal expenses are covered by a handful of partners who give on a monthly basis, so 100% of our church offerings go into our crusade expenses. Every dollar we receive from book sales and offerings goes into the ministry as well. My board has voted for me to receive a certain salary and the amount of my salary remains the same regardless of the size of our offerings.

You are your ministry. Without you there is no ministry. The workman is worthy of his hire. However, the needs of the ministry always come first. We have sacrificed personally many times so that we could do more ministry overseas.

What are some of the challenges that face a traveling minister? For the traveling minister, booking speaking engagements at churches has become harder in the last few years. In the past, churches used to have weeklong revivals, Sunday night services, missions conferences, and multi-day seminars. But now, with the busyness of America, many churches only have a Sunday morning service and a mid-week Bible study. American Christians simply do not go to church as much as they used to.

Since pastors like preaching, many pastors reserve the Sunday morning service for themselves. If they do invite a guest speaker, many pastors often invite another pastor to swap pulpits.

Another problem is that church services have become much

shorter. At one church, after worship songs, announcements, and the offering, the pastor turned to me and said, "Can you be finished preaching in seventeen minutes? My people will start leaving if we do not let the congregation out in time for them to beat other churches to the restaurant." Of course, I spoke for seventeen minutes, but after traveling for many hours to get to his church, I felt my message was severely cut short. It is hard to build people's faith for a life-changing miracle in only seventeen minutes.

Is there a place for traveling ministers in today's church? Unfortunately, some pastors have developed a deep mistrust of traveling ministers. At some conferences, I have witnessed pastors mock traveling ministers. They say, "Traveling ministers are just looking for a meeting." This is because some ministers may have abused the pastor's pulpit by demanding huge offerings, promising a certain level of blessing that does not materialize, and aggressively asking church members to partner with his ministry.

The truth is that the body of Christ needs every type of ministry. Paul said, *"He Himself gave some to be apostles, some prophets, some evangelists, and some pastors and teachers"* (Ephesians 4:11). If the body of Christ is going to be fully equipped, every ministry gift is needed. Notice that pastors come fourth on this list. Their role in the local church is only one-fifth of what God needs in the local church.

As an evangelist, I am not looking for a meeting or an offering; I am looking for a soul to be saved. As long as I keep soulwinning my primary focus, God provides the places for me to speak. Others might have tarnished the traveling ministry by acting dishonorably, but the best way for you to redeem the traveling ministry is by choosing to behave honorably, to minister with a servant's heart, and to genuinely help pastors accomplish something great for God.

Conclusion

There are huge needs in the world today. Marriages are falling apart. Bodies are sick. Families face economic difficulties. Teenagers are rebelling against the teachings of the Bible. Churches face declining membership. Pastors are discouraged. Critics mock the body of Christ. Because of all these problems, the world needs your ministry more than ever before.

Believe in yourself and the call of God on your life. Believe that the same God who called you will favor you with open doors to speak at churches. I encourage you to apply the principles in this book to your ministry. As you build relationships, you will never lack for a place to minister.

The harvest is plentiful, but the laborers are few. Because you have chosen to be a laborer for God's kingdom, you will experience amazing harvest in your life and ministry.

If there is ever anything we can do to serve you, please let us know.

Your co-laborers in the harvest fields,

Daniel + Jessica King

Our Goal?
Every Soul!

Daniel & Jessica King

About the Author

Daniel King and his wife Jessica met in the middle of Africa while they were both on a mission trip. They are in high demand as speakers at churches and conferences all over North America. Their passion, energy, and enthusiasm are enjoyed by audiences everywhere they go.

They are international missionary evangelists who do massive soul-winning festivals in countries around the world. Their passion for the lost has taken them to over fifty nations preaching the gospel to crowds that often exceed 50,000 people.

Daniel was called into the ministry when he was five years old and began to preach when he was six. His parents became missionaries to Mexico when he was ten. When he was fourteen he started a children's ministry that gave him the opportunity to minister in some of America's largest churches while still a teenager.

At the age of fifteen, Daniel read a book where the author encouraged young people to set a goal to earn $1,000,000. Daniel reinterpreted the message and determined to win 1,000,000 people to Christ every year.

Daniel has authored thirteen books including his best sellers *Healing Power*, *The Secret of Obed-Edom*, and *Fire Power*. His book *Welcome to the Kingdom* has been given away to tens of thousands of new believers.

Soul Winning Festivals

Metu, Ethiopia

Khushpur, Pakistan

Roca Blanca, Mexico

Sialkot, Pakistan

Agere Maryam, Ethiopia

Kisaran, Indonesia

When Daniel King was fifteen years old, he set a goal to lead 1,000,000 people to Jesus before his 30th birthday. Instead of trying to become a millionaire, he decided to lead a million "heirs" into the kingdom of God. *"If you belong to Christ then you are heirs"* (Galatians 3:29).

After celebrating the completion of this goal, Daniel & Jessica made it their mission to go for one million souls every year.

This **Quest for Souls** is accomplished through:

* Soul Winning Festivals
* Leadership Training
* Literature Distribution
* Humanitarian Relief

Would you help us lead
people to Jesus by joining
The MillionHeir's Club?

Visit www.kingministries.com to get involved!

MASTER SOUL WINNER

Learn practical tips on sharing your faith with friends and family.

$10.00

SOUL WINNING

Do you have a passion for the lost? This book shares over 150 truths about soul winning.

$10.00

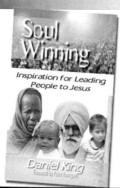

WELCOME TO THE KINGDOM

This is a perfect book for new believers. Learn how to be saved, healed, and delivered.(Available in bulk discounts)

$10.00

THE POWER SERIES

HEALING POWER

Do you need healing? This power-packed book contains 17 truths to activating your healing today!

$20.00

FIRE POWER

Inside these pages you will learn how to CATCH the fire of God, KEEP the fire of God, and SPREAD the fire of God!

$12.00

POWER OF THE SEED

Discover the power of Seedtime & Harvest! Discover why your giving is the most important thing you will ever do!

$20.00

KING MINISTRIES INTERNATIONAL

TOLL FREE: 1-877-431-4276
PO BOX 701113
TULSA, OK 74170 USA

ORDER ONLINE:
WWW.KINGMINISTRIES.COM

WRITE A BOOK

* Why you should write a book.
* How to put your ideas on paper.
* Ways to overcome writer's block.
* Secrets of Editing, Designing, Publishing, and Marketing Your Book.

$12.00

RAISING MONEY

* 10 Secrets of Raising Money for your Ministry.
* How to finance the vision God has given you.
* Why it is more important to be a "friend-raiser than a "fund-raiser."

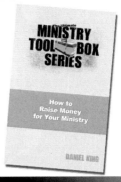

$12.00

BOOKING SPEAKING ENGAGEMENTS

For the last ten years, Daniel King has ministered an average of one hundred times every year in North America. In this short but explosive book written for traveling ministers he shares the secrets that will help you succeed in the traveling ministry!

$12.00

 **KING** MINISTRIES INTERNATIONAL

TOLL FREE: 1-877-431-4276
PO BOX 701113
TULSA, OK 74170 USA

ORDER ONLINE:
WWW.KINGMINISTRIES.COM

The vision of King Ministries is to lead 1,000,000 people to Jesus every year and to train believers to become leaders.

To contact Daniel & Jessica King:

Write:
King Ministries International
PO Box 701113
Tulsa, OK 74170 USA

King Ministries Canada
PO Box 3401
Morinville, Alberta T8R 1S3 Canada

Call toll-free:
1-877-431-4276

Visit us online:
www.kingministries.com

E-Mail:
daniel@kingministries.com